THE WORLD

IS GOD'S

LANGUAGE

Dear Vanessa,

Thank you for featuring some
of these poems in The Dewdrop,
for your kind support,
and your practice.

Sincerely,

Dave

THE WORLD
IS GOD'S
LANGUAGE

Prose Poems

Dane Cervine

Sixteen Rivers Press

Special thanks to David Sibbet for his
support of Sixteen Rivers Press

Published by Sixteen Rivers Press
P.O. Box 640663
San Francisco, CA 94164-0663
www.sixteenrivers.org

ISBN: 978-1-939639-26-4
Library of Congress
Control Number: 2020942638

Quotation, page 86: Sandra Meek, Editor,
*Deep Travel, Contemporary American Poets
Abroad*, Ninebark Press (2007);
used by permission.

Book design: Wayne Smith

CONTENTS

Bali

World

Colors of the Underworld

PREFACE

I would like to acknowledge my debt to Gary Young, the prose-poem maestro living in Santa Cruz, California. His pioneering work has helped to shape a Japanese-style short form, a kind of blended American haiku and *haibun* in prose-poem format, creating a new poetic focus for Western poets and readers.

Other influences on my work include Simone Weil, French philosopher, mystic, and political activist, who wrote "Attention is prayer"—a perspective that fills these pages—and the Buddhist teacher Kukai, who taught that the world is made up of a pictoral alphabet of image-letters (*monji*), spelling out the universe-body to any who would read it.

Poetry is a way of reading this world.

—Dane Cervine, Santa Cruz, California

HISTORIES

Experience is never limited, and it is never complete; it is an immense sensibility, a kind of huge spider-web . . .
—Henry James, "The Art of Fiction"

⚬

Seize the moments of happiness, love and be loved! That is the only reality in the world, all else is folly.
—Leo Tolstoy, *War and Peace*

Breast

It was in some obscure motel room, cheap, and I was young. But there it was, luminous orb falling from my mother's bra as she changed clothes in close quarters. I had no memory of infant days—swell of milk, suckle of nipple—no glimpse of the days yet to come. All I knew, in one moment, was how it begins: the shape of loss, its sweet curve.

Secret Lover

I wake wrapped in my own arms, hand having found bare shoulder under shirt. Embarrassed, I start to withdraw my limbs, but then linger in this embrace. Who else could love me from the inside out?

Mystery of the Locked Door

I remember Saturday morning cartoons, watching Coyote chase Roadrunner while my parent's bedroom door remained locked. But one morning, *surprise!* They emerge giggling, father chasing mother down the hallway, around the kitchen, with a huge zucchini squash held between his legs. So unusual in our house, but it made me happy: secret joy spilling out from behind the locked door.

Communion

My father was a preacher. At age five, I was too embarrassed to follow the others to the altar where he gave communion, but afterward my body crumpled into his as he soothed, brought me alone behind the choir benches, the organ, the towering cross, to the room where bits of bread remained on the silver tray, a few tiny shot glasses still filled with grape juice. I hungered for him, my remote father dressed in Sunday black—so when he pressed the crumbs into my hand, the purple stain to my lips, said, *This is my body, this is my blood,* I took him inside, believing.

Old World

Uncle Bob used to visit us at Sandy Acres: our handful of almond trees, old barn, scattered chickens and goats, on the outskirts of town. My parents had become teachers, dabbled at farming between dips in the pool and nightly television. But Uncle Bob was a true rancher, a navy man—had seen the dead, the sunken ships, the roosters running in the dirt, headless. When he came to visit, he knew only one way to live: take a chicken firmly in hand, pluck head from body, feather from skin, wash thighs and breast for the oven, bring meat to the table. And to my eyes: a world bruised with wonder.

Salvation's Weight

It was in Bible school, I was just old enough to sit with the adults, watch my father, see how it was done. When it came to God, my father had a true feeling for the matter—his face would squinch up, one eye would close, and he'd speak as though dragging heavy buckets up from a deep well. *We are saved by grace, not works . . .* but it seems like work, this grace in the cavernous dark. Lifting each excavated word to light, watching it evaporate in the air.

Fifth-Grade Lessons

Mr. Rivera with the golden ruler—he'd pace the classroom, sly smile and gleaming instrument poised to keep us in line or wake us up. Like a Zen master in a black and white suit, he'd begin a classic story, meander till we finally noticed the shift to superheroes battling villains. Or the time when half of us were daydreaming, his whisper to those listening: *Stay seated when I yell to stand up!* And there I was, standing so tall, proud, smiling.

Still Swimming

When I was twelve, I woke one morning, stepped into the backyard to play with our ten collie pups. So small, their orange-red fur would glisten in the sun as they gnawed my fingers, licked my face. But that night, they'd escaped the house, fallen into the swimming pool. Eight floated so still I knew I'd never recover. Reaching down, I pulled out the last two paddling by the cement lip—learning with each stroke how one survives.

Taking My Time

In the junior high boys' bathroom, I stumbled on two friends ogling a torn page from *Playboy*. Craning my neck round their shoulders, I stared at the naked woman, her flirtatious smile, the curve of breasts—turned, ran back outside to play because it was too soon. The way, now, I shrug my shoulders at death, seductive pout flickering across her soft face—how you never recover from that kind of loving.

Closer Than Imagined

The old cabin on the edge of town creaked and swayed in the wind, three of us sitting cross-legged on the floor round a flickering candle. We gathered to pray, to stir a storm of longing—adolescent hearts sure salvation was imminent.

After years of disappointment, I find it closer now than imagined: this heart, still fire, beyond any saving.

Some Prayers Are Better Left Unanswered

Back from college, lying beneath the body-length ceiling poster in the little room over the garage, I stared at the burgundy robe still shaped by the torso just ascended, doves escaping the collar. I longed to leave the body—truculent, misfitted—behind.

Praying to the poster, I reached toward its clouds, angelic light, wind—but found nothing I could drink, eat, sleep with. So I rose, passing instead into these long years of kissing the earth's stained body, her fickle hands, her dark ruby lips.

Bruised

When I was twenty, I started work at a psychiatric ward. After three summers in the tomato cannery, the mending of bruised minds appealed. No rejects crushed into paste: each red heart cupped, soothed, repaired. But on my first day, the nurse whispered that the head psychiatrist had hanged himself at home that morning. There are hidden blows; you must first save yourself.

The Foot-Washing Ceremony

It was dark. The deep purple carpet led from aisle to altar at the Methodist church, candles rimming the circular wooden border before the dais. There, removing shoes, socks, embarrassments, I sat in a simple chair, placed feet in the ritual bowl of clear water, allowed the person in front of me to gently wash each foot, then towel dry, then bow. Folding into the kneeling posture after, I turned, took the next two luminous, bashful feet into my hands like shy animals.

Green Revelation

Peter, our counterculture Sunday School teacher, taught the secret life of plants, how to see their auras, rather than Jesus dying for our sins. Perhaps this was true revelation: life, not in heaven, not in hell, but in every green thing.

Always Arriving

I remember that blazing California summer, just home from college—my parents lounging by the pool reading metaphysics. Peter and I, naked, playing guitars nearby, his wife, Ronda, singing a lyrical ditty: *See the children dancing in the forest, do they know, do they remember . . .* and the seventies sparkled with innocence, and the New Age was upon us. My father wondered, unsure if this was it, what we'd all been looking for, and I said, *Yes.* Never again to be so sure: this sweet doubt, the way it lingers over every happiness.

Mining What Matters

The wooden ore crusher stood three stories high outside the mine. With a bid to clear it all away, Peter tore the beams down, built a cabin on his own hillside. Massive, it was to be his last stand, a place of arrival. But life moves on, and he with it—tearing the cabin down, reconstructing smaller versions in each new backyard. Finally, all that was left: an empty place to sit. Inside this, a world.

The Measure of Desire

At age twenty—my first days working at the hospital—I met a man distressed that his engorged penis would not shrink. My job was to measure it every few hours, and for the next three days I leaned the wooden ruler against his phallus, counted the inches. In the end, relieved at his shrinking rod, he returned home. It was my first lesson in the limits of desire, the longing for less rather than more.

Litany of Desire

In college, I attended a psychology class where the professor had us identify as many names as possible for *penis, vagina, breast, testicle.* The lists were long—crude and elegant, full of gutter talk, ethereal allusions. These are the words, he said, you'll hear over and over as you counsel others. You must not flinch. You must not laugh. You must understand every phrase, the secret pain, the hidden longing. So we recited from the chalkboard, aloud and in unison, a human litany of pleasure and shame: *dick, boob, snatch, pussy, balls, melons, my flower, my better man, my reason for being.*

Rainbow Gathering

Modoc County, California, 1985

After graduate school, my brother took me to a remote corner of Nevada, where we pitched our tent next to a pair of rainbow women: nude except for a feather here, a crystal there. Democratic latrine pits in the open air, no one able to hide their shit. Food for the asking, mushrooms, spirits. After, not a shred of garbage left anywhere. But it was the circle at dusk, a mile-wide circumference of *Om* that still haunts—how at the edge of the meadow the plateau plummeted far down toward a town below. I live with this memory like a ghost limb.

News from Burning Man

Black Rock Desert, Nevada, the new millennium

After forty-mile-an-hour dust storms, water simply turns your body ashen. Thirty thousand techno-anarchists, some of them neighbors from back home, offer to paint your penis, cheek, torso in colors the desert only dreams of. The bottomless night is when the real work begins, pursuing Dionysus down endless tunnels the devil himself has yet to conceive. But when the Wicker Man burns—huge tower of corporate cardboard lit in the dead of night—you hope that the world may never be saved.

The Second Coming

The old-timer—two missing front teeth—leans into the field, whistles loudly for his horse, calling his name, *Jesus! Jesus!*, over and over till the aging stallion appears, trots toward the red apple in his hand. All these years—wild prayers to a hidden god—and this simple secret of ripe fruit, its scent, calling.

Aura

In Tahoe after skiing, Peter brings his latest find: an aura camera from Russia. When I place my finger on the receptacle, the computer screen displays fingers radiating energy—then my body emanating its aura. Taking my finger away, I'm not sure which is more unsettling: that my body burns with such light, or that it doesn't.

Growing Old

Redwood grove in the coastal range: two prodigious elders fused into a single trunk, burned hollow at the base from some disaster. Yet the tree still grows. Blackened redwood walls rise, a ruined cathedral, room enough for our small band to wander in, succumb to awe. I can feel how it happens: growing old around the burn, room now to shelter, sun drawing you where you want to go.

Surprise!

The big oak is down. It fell slowly, shallow roots easing the great giant across the Japanese garden into the snow without a sound. My mother, working in the forest a short distance away, returned to find the behemoth fallen *just so*—her house intact, one Buddha statue sitting serenely next to the huge trunk, another with its head knocked off beside the broken *torri* gate.

Trusting the World

Winter morning, visiting my aging mother in her forest home. I step into the outdoor redwood shower, close the wooden sliding door. Down falls a tiny black bat, wakened from sleep. Pummeled by the steaming water till my hand can reach the knob, it looks as befuddled as I am. Enfolding the wet bat in a towel, I lay it outside on the deck, watch it shudder, its pulsing lungs work, its small wings weakly stretch. Later, after a walk past the fallen oak, the trickling snowmelt, the hazy sun's warmth, I return to find the deck empty. Trusting that the bat has become prey for cat, or found its way again under the dark eaves.

Another Kind of Truth

Aunt Suzanne died in the early morning, the last stage of Alzheimer's ending with a sigh. Her gray matter resting now, after the kaleidoscopic firing of random neurons, memories, the confused details of a life blurring indiscriminately—where a banana is indeed a hammer or a husband, and death another kind of living.

Grateful Breadheads

A cabal of girls rush laughing into our house with loaves of sourdough bread perched on their heads like ritual caps. My daughter joins them, sitting cross-legged on the floor chanting *Om*, answering philosophical questions I pose to them. In their wisdom, each answer is the same: paradox, then uproarious laughter. And I wonder how they happened on the secret so young?

The Secret Work

The Burning Band on the Pacific Garden Mall drums unrelenting beats on upturned industrial containers, matched by ecstatic Hare Krishna chanters dancing alongside at the corner. I sway with my children as the drum sticks ricochet and pound. Across the circle, a young man in a black T-shirt, the white words on his chest, *Keep Santa Cruz Weird*, a whirling prayer—and I feel it, this life in the margins keeping the world's weight spinning.

In My Dreams

An old girlfriend suddenly appears. It is a narrow hallway in a lesbian bar, and we are both stunned to find each other again. Once sick and depressed, she is now my muse, kisses me fiercely. As though we had never failed life once, as though we'd found a way to live in the world rather than dream.

*

In the city, I was not afraid this time of the tattooed young men lurking ominously on the corner. Instead, I looked into their eyes and smiled. One stepped forward, pierced his chest with a long metal staple, then popped it in the air with one flex of his bulging pectoral. We laughed at how strength bides its time, waits for something important to do.

*

I was not embarrassed, ambling through the sex shop, taking my time with every novelty. No furtive hovering, no concealed wishes. Stepping to the counter, I announced eagerly to the proprietor, *I'll take one of everything!*

The World a House

The sign reads "World Cultures at San Juan Bautista" as I drive to see my brother, who has just returned from New Zealand, Thailand, Bali, with his new handmade guitar from a folk festival in Australia. A thousand notes play on his heart, a music of the world so wide there is no telling if any one place can ever be large enough for him to call home.

Householding

Eventually, my wandering brother buys a house. Having seen corrugated tin shanties, thatched huts by the Pacific, the way women come and go, the heart so unclear, he caresses the timbers of his first home like a lover. Like a body he could spend the rest of his life inside.

The Conjuror

My youngest brother became a magician, traveled the world winning prizes. My father built him a hexagon all his own, with floor-to-ceiling mirrors to practice in front of. When Father died, my brother became a filmmaker, capturing in images what he could not conjure from the empty box: not just memory, but love's real body.

The Sound of One Hand Waving

My sister visited Hawaii one year, following the footsteps of our mother when young. An aunt, who survived Pearl Harbor's carnage. The Big Island became home for my sister, too, when the man on the beach offered his heart. Her three brothers and her parents still on the mainland. There is sometimes grief in every joy. Which is why she became a hula dancer, I suspect: *aloha* signifying greeting *and* parting. The one impossible word of it.

Angels

Mother tells us of her drive home from the airport, a flat tire along the road—hints at feeling old, unsure. How two young Mexican men stopped, helped her change tires, refused any money. In her story, the disenfranchised watch over each other—like guardian angels who know what it means to fall.

The Unseen

My wife circles the winter pond in Madison, Indiana, having spent the day with her father in the adjacent nursing home. He knows his daughter, but grabs at thin air to touch a fruit tree, a dog, a tombstone no one else can see. Marvels as she walks right through them. She tells me this as her words rise invisibly through the cold steam of her breath to travel via cell phone towers to my ear in California. Though I can't see her, I know she is there.

Already Dying

My cells are dying. Every inch of my skin, already deceased. Several billion tiny fragments are sloughed off each day. Running a finger along the dusty shelf: I am drawing a pattern on my old self.

Hope

She feeds herself bone-marrow soup, beef heart, while carcinoma spreads its white gossamer through her body. Acupuncture, Reiki, herbs—soon, the surgeon's hands. How delicately they will search for what can be taken, pray over what cannot.

Her two cats saved from the hurricane's aftermath tussle and play in sun-drenched rooms, then curl in a basket dreaming of storm, of her soft, delicate fingers.

Match Point

After hearing the diagnosis—liver and pancreatic cancer—my uncle went out on the tennis court at seventy-eight years of age, played the last match of his life, won. Forty-nine days later, death took him at *love.*

Practicing

I'm practicing dying, he said to his daughter in his last days. *I slowly stop breathing to see what it's like, then let go.* His words almost eager: *I think I can do this*—the way a young boy steadies himself on the cliff bank over a river, gnarled rope in hand, leaps.

Anniversary

He tries twice to leave for Peru to visit the site in the remote Andes where his parents' plane crashed. First, the flight circles back after an hour for security reasons. Then another plane: an engine blows, returns to land. He is beside himself. As though the place he would visit in his heart can be reached only this way.

Beyond the River

At the end of a glorious week by the Russian River, our friends receive a call from extended family: a twenty-seven-year-old son, gone. Unclear whether it was the heroin, or his liver from drinking. I walk onto the deck, let them finish. Pick up yesterday's paper for distraction—the London subway bombings, how it was always a matter of *when*, not *if*.

The Black Slippers

After my father died, I brought one pair of his black flip-flop slippers home with me. The first time I wear them, my son comments, *Those were Grandpa's!* Looks at me as though, by this small act, I am bringing him to life again, the *clop-clop* across the tiled kitchen floor an aural reincarnation. I tell him when next we visit Grandma, I'll show him a secret. Already, I can see him opening the shed door, tilting the brown grocery bag filled to the brim with black slippers, watching them spill across the floor as a path, for both of us, to walk on.

Looking Forward

Her grandpapa and nana sit at breakfast in Madison, Indiana, talk about the latest doctor visit—his pacemaker in need of recalibration—and in her eyes I see how old we seem. But in the next breath, stories of their trip to China, being carried on the backs of elephants—her eyes wide, the world a playground for those who know its mysteries. After, in the parking lot, she spins in the summer rain, arms raised, tongue extended, soaking in every last drop.

Full Moon Rising

Mom slips into the spa with her wine cooler, recalls the movie she saw at the foreign film theater downtown: *Mother*. About an older woman who loses her husband, moves in with her children, and forgets she has a life. Then, a brief affair with a hired hand—her body remembering—and she's off, pursuing a new destiny.

My mother laughs when I ask about the guy working on her house. Says friendship is better than a man, less trouble. The moons of her eyes so bright.

Aspiration

Four older women gather for breakfast at the next table adjacent, chatting up a storm. Energetic, they seem in the prime of their lives, gray hair shimmering against tan and white sweaters. Outside the bakery window, most leaves have fallen from the maple—but handfuls of color rustle on spare limbs. There is so much room now, and you can see the sky.

Stirring Life's Cup

I sit with Mother at the café after Father's surgery, not knowing the future, but thinking how beautiful, how brave she seems—more herself than she's ever been. Life so liquid as we pour milk into blackness, stir—in each cup: the richest mahogany color.

World Yoga

Yoga in the outdoor Pagoda hexagon with my eighty-year-old mother. The thin summer screen decorated with orange and green butterflies keeps the bugs out, still lets the world in.

A smiling stone Buddha watches every move. Six gunshots echo from a rifle in the hills—a hunter stalking squirrel, birds, even deer? My mother doesn't mind. Death, she says, is just another way the world moves.

The Story of a Marriage

My wife married a poet, which is no safe journey. Like Osiris, lost to the underworld, bones and ligaments scattered, hidden in spells, drowned at the river's bottom. Like Isis, she scours the wilderness for every lost part—knits me together anew. All this, while being queen of her own domain. It takes an immense story to tell a mortal tale. How though I am flayed, flawed, she'll listen while I knead her divine shoulders, dig my thumbs beneath each blade.

BALI

I know that the surface of water hides a parallel world.
—Ito Naga, *I Know*

⌒

We see by means of something which illumines us, which we do not see.
—Antonio Porchia, *Voices*

The World Is God's Language

—Simone Weil

Andi tells us how the best coffee in Bali comes from beans eaten by a fox, passed through undigested, roasted, sold at exorbitant prices. That the whole banana tree is used for food, baskets, prayers. Everything in Bali has both use and spirit. Even the careening motor scooters. At the curb, adorned with bamboo prayer baskets, filled with red hibiscus petals.

Sometimes the Gods Sing So Loud I Can't Hear

Green cicadas the size of thumbs announce the coming dusk with deafening sound in the trees near our balcony. Their small chests expand and contract rapidly, breast armor creating sound akin to immense electric saws. The cicadas loose their ear-splitting sound only when it is quiet—and always just before dark. I press my thumbs to both ears. God's music, deafening.

Embracing the World

Outside my window in the Bali hills: green rice fields. In the distance, Java's coastline. I have come halfway round the world seeking quiet in the mountain village of Munduk, though my quest is elusive. Each morning, the farmer's wife begins her day-long task of scaring crows from the field by yanking a long string tied to a rusted coffee can, hung like a bell with a fork inside. *Clang-clang, clang-clang! Clang-clang!*

The Embrace

The two old Frenchmen wave at each other across the Balinese veranda, then embrace, one firm kiss on each cheek, intimate, earthy. Unapologetic. Like the children outside dressed only in their skin, walking arm around waist down the dirt road. At home in their bodies, as though they are not just visiting.

The Fate of Prayers

The roots of the banyan tree are slowly engulfing the stone floor of the small temple the tree grows in the center of. The tree itself is swallowing the old black-and-white checkered cloth representing the yin and yang of life—and the gray squares where they overlap in the human. Still, each day, new gifts appear on the ancient steps: flower petals in bamboo trays, a slice of melon, a tangle of grass.

Invisible Threads

The old man on his haunches, scythe in hand, cuts tufts of grass handful by handful near the rice fields. Ten kites of gold and red float in wind far overhead, the strings that tie them to earth invisible from here.

The Third Face of God

The orange cat sits on the orange stone, peering through green bamboo at Lord Shiva chiseled into the clay-block wall. Without belief, she knows well Shiva's predilection for divine destruction: mouse bones to mulch, rain to mud, breath to silence. She turns to lick her wild fur, eyes the careless cricket singing in the leaves.

Interpreting the Body

Down a quiet alley in Bali, lying prone on a massage table, I peer through the wooden hole cupping my face, become the oblong brown bowl filled with water and red petals beneath. A woman's thumbs, elbows, and palms find the pain in me that hides inside shoulders, spine, feet. Does God search me as ardently as she seeks out the pain? Is She here now, in the room, touching my body with wonder, my wounded heart, saying, *What is this pain here, and here, and here?*

A Balinese Tale of the Tortoise and the Hare

Andi, our trekking guide through the terraced rice fields in the northern mountains of Bali, eyes me thoughtfully. He worked in London for a year, returning because the pace of life was so harried: *No one had time to even say hello. So much stress!* I tell him we Americans are even more stressed than the Europeans, and his eyes grow large. We continue in silence through the green fields, toward a finish line neither of us yet sees, but which only one of us is chasing.

The Sex Life of Vanilla Plants

Vanilla! he says, pointing to the spent vines strung in rows across the hillside. The Balinese farmer says there would not be vanilla but for humans, because there are no bees in Bali that can pollinate its flowers. Farmers go from plant to plant, use the thorn of the snakeskin fruit tree to open the vanilla flowers and press the female part to the male. So here is the proof: We too are part of nature, conceived by vanilla as matchmaker and voyeur.

Seeing Is Believing

Over breakfast by the Bali Sea, I read Bashō, Rilke, Kabir, silently ecstatic. My son, after much thought, complains that the pancakes are too bland, the toast inadequate, the milk too thick. I begin laughing, to his dismay. After all, the world is true to our complaint, confirms every inadequacy, yields to our estimation. The eyes are mirrors.

The Politics of Harmony

By a pond in Bali, huge frogs thunder their opera each night. They intone two distinct notes, a call and response. But sometimes a rebel will croak off-key, or choose a different note to bellow. The other frogs bully it away till the symphony again finds its chord. Is this how Lucifer was spurned, his solo at odds with celestial music? Always the same perfect notes, endlessly repeated?

The Interpenetration of Worlds

I watch the blue dragonfly flit over the koi pond time and again, as if mesmerized by the orange and white fish beneath. A world thicker than air, a depth it cannot fathom. The koi, in return, must catch sight of a strange blur from another world, one above, beyond. Sitting silently adjacent, I see both realms. The koi, the dragonfly— and the human, many worlds in one. Who is it, then, inside this silence, watching me?

Strange Beauty

Our Bali guide brushes his hand over the bark of the jackfruit tree, shows us knife marks children have made. They collect the sap that oozes from the wound on long thin branches, then stalk dragonflies. After, they run laughing to mothers with their delicious prisoners, roast them over coals, pop crackling dragons into open mouths. It is a lush world—each wound a strange beauty.

WORLD

I would ask something more of this world if it had something more.

　　　—Antonio Porchia, *Voices*

I know that once the eyelids are closed, the eyes go on seeing.

　　　— Ito Naga, *I Know*

Starting Over in 1803

Every evening, the Boston-born Sir David Ochterlony would take all thirteen of his Indian consorts around Delhi, each on the back of her own elephant.

Eros Finds a Way

Centuries ago, Muslims came to Hindu India. Suspicious of sexuality, they divided mind from body, the sensual from the metaphysical. Somehow, the long Indian tradition of eros was not disturbed. Inspired by the *Kama Sutra*, Muslim weavers shed their heavy black burkas and created delicate fabrics of translucent magenta, pale pink. Lovers would step into *baft hawa* ("woven air"), *ab-e-rawan*, ("running water"), *shabnam* ("evening dew"). The weavers, secret mystics clothing this body with light.

Ghosts in Eden

In the Amazon there are fruit trees: sapodilla, calabash, tucumá, babcçu, wild pineapple, coco palm. The ranger says visitors are amazed at nature's abundance, how you can walk in the forest and pick fruit from wild trees. But he tells them it's because someone planted them. They're walking through ancient orchards.

Anti-Mass

Anti-Mass: a wood charcoal, nails, and wire sculpture by Cornelia Parker

Charred remains of a Southern Baptist Church destroyed by arsonists hang from the ceiling of the art museum, blackened board fragments suspended in air by wire in a perfect rectangle, defying gravity, floating as a miraculous spectral object: the lost church. The bodily presence of its congregation made more powerful by absence. The sign reads, "Mass: elemental substance of the universe and the sacramental ritual at the center of Christian faith." This blackened sculpture an anti-Mass, then. Nails still embedded in the wood.

Legacy

Niangara is an old trading post at the confluence of two rivers in the Congo. During Belgian rule, it was a boomtown for cotton and coffee, though you would never know that now. Roofless old Belgian houses sink into elephant grass, the once paved roads now gluey mud. A group of skinny men on bicycles. In the red dirt, huge leafy trees are crowded with mangos. Children are told to rub themselves with palm kernel oil as a shield against bullets. They are the only soldiers left.

The Parable of St. Matthew Island

The Coast Guard brought twenty-nine reindeer to this island in the Bering Sea as a backup food supply for the nineteen soldiers stationed there. After World War II, the base was closed. Thirteen years later, a thousand reindeer fed on the four-inch-thick mat of lichen that covered the island, then six thousand a decade later. In just three more years, travelers found only a small herd, not much lichen, and fields of reindeer skeletons. Soon, it was only skeletons.

The Dreams of Antelope

In Yellowstone, wolves were reintroduced into the mountains and then fed again on the antelope, which stopped over-eating the willow trees, so the birds returned to sing and beavers started making dams again from the fallen branches, resurrecting the marshes, and once more everything started turning green because a wild predator was allowed back into the dreams of antelope.

Shaking Penises

The immigrant boy from the Philippines smiled, raised his hand, said *Yes* when the teacher asked if anyone had ever touched his private parts. Worried by the boy's eager admission, a social worker investigated, removed him from his home. After months of court testimony, appeals, it was deemed a cultural mistake: a tribal ritual, this greeting of young boys by shaking their penises. The now frightened boy returned to his father, his uncles and grandfathers, who no longer knew how to honor his manhood in this country—grasping instead his limp hands, shaking each one as a foreign language.

Tyrannies

My daughter tells her story of traveling by train to Prague with several citizens who remembered food under the communist regime. There were no choices, not like in America. You bought *milk, eggs, bread,* and it was oddly freeing. No endless brand names to labor over, just the simple, good thing itself.

Out of Our Minds

Oeno and Ducie Islands are atolls in the South Pacific—uninhabited, remote. Still, garbage drifts from Asia and the Americas thousands of miles distant: plastic bags, Suntory whisky bottles, rope, shoes, lightbulbs, toy soldiers, bike pedals, screwdrivers. The effluvia of paradise.

Gated Communities

Maya kings, Norse Greenland lords, Easter Island chiefs—in the long run, they merely bought the privilege of being the last to starve. When the final Brazilian forest is gone, the Arctic melt lapping our porches, sweet air sour everywhere, who will punch the last code into the last pointless gate—opening, then closing with a final bolted *clank*?

Erosion of Faith

In Iowa, a church was built in the middle of farmland during the nineteenth century. One hundred and fifty years later, the churchyard now stands like a small island ten feet above the eroding sea of fields: a beacon, a tombstone.

Dinosaurs

Driving down the street, I observe vehicles of every shape, size, color meandering around town, feeding at gas stations, mingling oblivious to imminent extinction, like dinosaurs grazing wide tropical plains. This is how it must have been—such gorgeous hunger lifting its head, a shift in temperature, a grand eon slipping imperceptibly away. I stroke the steering wheel's round neck, its long column disappearing beneath the floorboard, say, *Don't despair, I will remember you.*

Offering

Venice, city of 118 islands, is sinking. But what a beauty while she lasts. I wander the labyrinth of alleys, stare at the green patina of the copper-roofed cathedral, sit on moss-covered steps lapped by the Adriatic. You can almost feel her going under: the slow pull of it, this offering of your life, stone by stubborn stone, to the rising sea.

Broken Desire

Pope Pius IX decided the sight of male genitalia on sculpture might incite lust—so with chisel and mallet, had the penises of every male statue inside Vatican City hacked off. Works by Michelangelo, Bramante, Bernini—hundreds of fig leaves now covering each emasculation. As though desire could be eviscerated from our bodies—or covered by such tender, slender leaves.

Magellan's Voyage Around the World

When the last biscuit was gone, they scraped the maggots out of the casks, mashed and served them as gruel. Then made cakes out of sawdust soaked with the urine of rats. The rats themselves, as delicacies, had long since been hunted to extinction. But oh!, the wonder of that unknown world, there, on the horizon—pineapple, mangos, hope—worth any distance, any deprivation.

Modern Hero

The blond-curled college kid stands alone on the roof, stares out to sea. His green baseball cap askew, his black Metallica T-shirt untucked, beer held absently between two fingers. The ocean, like his discontent, knows no bounds. He is measuring the quest, how far he must go—with no timber, no compass, no sail.

Prophecy

As I browse for calendars—images of Tibetan Buddhas, Frida's deer with a crown of thorns—a white-bearded street musician careens into the store shouting for pictures of the Virgin Mary, rails against the Machine, anguished that we don't open our eyes and *See!* He turns, glares at my silver whiskers, bellows, *Those with white beards are like gods rising from the depths to testify truth*—then storms out of the store, continuing his tirade. For only a moment, I am afraid he might be wrong about us.

Do I Wake or Sleep?

In my dream, Nietzsche emerges unshaven from a Nazi railroad car, empty now of its human cargo, announces that God is dead. Of course, the existentialist lived before Hitler, but history is a dream run backward, and dreams are a way of catching up with history. So I tell him, as I wake, that he promised a *superman* in his future—a human marvel that God's death would make room for. But he only sighs, points his weary finger at me as I disappear, wake again into this world of sleeping gods.

The Hairdresser Knows It Is the Self
We Seek to Shape

At the entrance to his shop, he watches the rain with cigarette dangling from lip, coffee cup in hand. A gruff sort, heavyset, goatee—a guru waiting for that first man, that first woman, to trundle in from the wildness outside, hair askew, say, *Just a trim,* or *Off, take it all off, I want something new!*

Looking for a Life

At the Walmart bargain movie bin, a young man with a five o'clock shadow sorts through the piles of films, one by one, looking for choice selections. His black tattooed bicep ripples as he pulls armfuls of adventure, drama, comedy onto the floor, examines each—tosses most back like fish too small to eat. Says, *Who needs to drink, or hang out at the bars,* when a world lies in your hand. Stepping outside, I finger my skull for the right button, push Play.

Keeping Watch

Bobbie was tall, lanky, lobotomized—synapse clipped from frontal lobe decades ago. Nights at the psych ward, I'd look in on him lying stiff under the sheets, murmur soothing words: *Lay your head down on the pillow, Bobbie, it's okay.* But he'd keep it aloft for hours, lying prone, rigid, watchful. I knew he was keeping an eye out for something, or against something—sometimes, in the middle of the long night, I would see it, too.

Union

They were married, both stricken with Alzheimer's, living together in one room at Harbor Hills. They would constantly try on clothes— he a skirt, she his shirt. Often his pants would end up on her arms; her shoes fit snugly over both his hands. What tragic grace, at the end of life together—so determined to fit each inside the other.

The World Looks Better in Black & White

The small burgundy house in San Rafael, home to six men with schizophrenia, brain chemistry awry. I lived there weekends to keep an eye on them. Cooked a whole pack of bacon with Ben, enough for invisible friends around the table. Chewed the fat with Steve, his fickle voices exalting one moment, demeaning the next.

At night, we'd watch old black and white television shows—*Father Knows Best, Leave It to Beaver*—where the world was redeemed by a plate of cookies, a pat on the back, a promise that tomorrow would be be better.

Strange Calculus

The blue BMW took the curve in poor geometry, a straight line, unbending, finding the hypotenuse of the parked Caltrans truck, then the orange-clad worker angling toward the stalled motorist along the roadside, intersected by what remained of the Highway Patrol officer's black motorcycle, multiplied by the carnage of odds, the equation of benign symmetry less than zero, a negative number—the way trees go on waving in the wind past any calculus.

Song of the World

Two men play cello and violin by the sea as pedestrians pass by,
though their music can barely be heard amid crashing surf, wind,
squawking seagulls. But with every arch of bow across string, the
entire tumult seems evoked note by note—while I wave my arms,
conduct the clamorous day.

Longing to Give Chase

At the beach, a golden retriever barks and claws at the large gray
rock partially submerged in wet sand. The waves surround them,
then recede, again and again. The dog barks, unrelenting—insisting
the rock move, find its legs, run.

Hobbies of the Gods

Two aging men in Cincinnati, their basement filled with miniature houses, rooms—and inside those: tiny books, shoes, fruit. As though life was an immensity so great it could only be held by the small, the particular.

The Dream of a Perfect Life

She speaks of their stock portfolios, the perfect house, the perfect life. Every detail of marriage—no children, lots of travel—plotted in the longitude and latitude of dream. The blush and rouge of her cheeks glow, the flawless line of lipstick and eye undeniable. Is this how God felt in the beginning, the gleam in Her eye before the devil in every detail made the real possible?

Transparent

A full ochre moon rises over the ridge by Cherry Lake, illuminates the smoke from lightning-strike fires drifting down currents of air into the valley. I sit at midnight in cool sand by the stream feeding the lake, quiet pools meandering for millennia. What it means to be human so transparent: belonging to smoke, fire, water, tree. Brain stem empty of chatter. Heart quiet and happy as a hen warming the perfect oval of desire.

The Empty Hand Holds the World

For the first five hundred years, the Buddha was represented by an empty seat, a tree with no one beneath it, a pair of footprints. *Tathāgata: one who has thus gone,* hence able to contain the whole world. Greek settlers in India turned him into a statue—a stone hero—rather than wind, or earthquake, or inconsolable rain.

The Broken Family in Paris

At La Closerie des Lilas, where Hemingway dined on bourbon-soaked steak, my daughter places one rough-cut slice in her mouth, which melts in dusky sweetness on her tongue. Surprised that something so dark and heavy can be so unbearably light, we four savor bites from one fork. Whiskey gravy on the lip, lilac petals falling through the open roof.

The Birth of the Modern World

That summer in Florence, Gertrude and Leo Stein lingered for hours stretched on the library floor of the Berensons' villa, smoking cigars and drinking lemonade. They were the unflappable American siblings about to turn Paris on its head. But what did they know, then, about modern art, Cubism, avant-garde literature? Perhaps only that the dusty classic books on the shelf seemed faded, the Grecian urn, the Roman bust too perfect. The lemonade tangy, irreverent. The cigar smoke turning everything queer, surreal, nouveau.

Self-Abuse in the Victorian Age

Gertrude Stein was admonished by her physician against masturbation, promoting, instead, premarital sex to ward off homosexuality—the apparent outcome of too much self-loving. Her brother, Leo, tried so hard that all erotic impulses were, literally, shoved into the fetish of a shoe. He'd no idea how much pathos one shoe could carry. No one could make much sense of the body's enigmatic mammalian roar, so a zoo seemed proper. Cages of various design, creed, buffoonery.

Gertrude knew something was wrong with this charade, as she had studied to be a doctor and had read Otto Weininger, the twenty-three-year-old gay Viennese Jew who hanged himself in the room where Beethoven died to protest just about everything. She gave his book to everyone she knew. Then openly began to love the woman she was mad about.

Because *the self* will out itself, one way or another—whether by hanging, spiked shoe, or immaculate, stubborn love.

The Anthropology of Memory

Death swallows all. The existentialists, particularly the French, understand. Still, there are the small rebellions. There is memory. Digging for the forgotten. Holding fragments in hand, lifting them into light.

So after Paris, I buy a used book cheap to remember the French existentialist Henri Michaux, who in turn remembers an Ecuadorian poet named Gangotena who was possessed of genius and ill luck— who died young, along with his poems, most of them unpublished, burned in a plane crash.

No internet search will find them. No Library of Congress hold them. The great library at Alexandria burned, and some future viral plague may yet take every word now saved in the world's memory banks with it into oblivion. Of course, there's always our own sun's eventual solar demise, against which all human arrogance, and every poem, will fail. Unless that beautiful arrogance finds us, somehow, a home on another world, a younger world, where Henri and I may yet reside side by side in gold or titanium memory chips, or even subtler clouds of data. But the Ecuadorian poet's poems are, despite all arrogance, despite love, forever lost. Except his name, Gangotena.

That he was a genius. That he had bad luck. That someone remembers.

I am just a visitor here

in this cathedral, mouth open and mute under the immense stone husk of the dome. Marveling at the intricate stained glass rich with purple hues, popes, martyrs. Hundreds of votive candles flicker in glass vases, the white tulips on green stems in clay pots, the wooden pews where I kneel, an unbeliever in all save the vaulted empty spaces, the sad eyes of Mary, how she doesn't look away.

The Duomo in Siena

Amid the clerics' call for quiet in the cathedral, two infants in baby carriages are strolled inside the cavernous silence, eyes immense, tiny mouths echoing each other: *Ah! Ah! Ah!*

COLORS OF THE UNDERWORLD

Even the smallest of creatures carries a sun in its eyes.

    —Antonio Porchia, *Voices*

Begat from paramecium and gingko trees,

My great, great grandfather an amoeba,

My grandmother a cherry blossom.

I will become rain.

    —Iwasaki Tsuneo, *Painting Enlightenment*

Finding Eden

Again in Bali, snorkeling the coral reefs of Indonesia, then wandering the temples of eastern Kyoto, I return home to find my own garden overrun. Rosebushes a tempest of dead buds, stone paths littered with weeds, spider webs strung from plum tree to fence in front of the serene Buddha. A snake lounging in the grass.

Year of Living Dangerously

In Jakarta, the Chinese Christian mayor is put on trial for blasphemy. Nearby, a Manila casino in the Philippines is attacked by gunmen. America's in the news here in Indonesia, too, for all the wrong reasons.

Still, just off the beach from my bungalow in Tomei, a vast coral reef is protected by two Swedish men who pay seventeen villages to fish elsewhere. We collect the Indonesian candy wrappers the tide brings each evening, tossed by children into the sea. The large sea turtle edges just out of sight in the deep blue. The octopus changes color underwater.

Evenings, I pound my keyboard like a piano. There are never enough notes for this world.

Indonesian Prayers

Off the island of Tomei at night, snorkeling the dark sea by flashlight, spying an octopus with its flurry of tentacles stirring sea dust—I surface, see the full moon nestled in its pitch-black tent of sky, hear the piercing *adhan* from the muezzin calling villagers to the mosque. I dive back into the dark sea.

Colors of the Underworld

Floating like a sea mammal off shore, my long fins and tight mask allow me to hover as though a bird in liquid sky. I am suddenly surrounded by hundreds of tiny black and yellow fish, their forked tails each a spear of Neptune, and I, a momentary captive of this deep.

Depth Perception

Madé, our Indonesian diving guide, says that before his intrepid Swedish friend came to build this preserve, he thought that the coral he now loves was merely razor-sharp rock. His people knew only how to fish to feed a family. Before I saw the families fish, I thought only of colorful coral, of saving the planet. The irony is not lost on us. It took a foreigner's eyes for each of us to *see* our own blindness.

Rubik's Cube of the Indian Ocean

The vanishing coral lives at the very seam where colonial Europe and native Indonesia meet. Laughing children scatter the candy wrappers Western business taught their elders to make, clogging waterways with bright colors. Marine scientists urge fishermen to keep their boats from eroding the coral, which turns its brilliant colors gray.

Without the scientists, the coral will vanish. Without the fishermen, Indonesia will starve. Without the children, joy will vanish.

Amaterasu

Goddess of the sun who created ancient Japan

Wandering through the Hiroshima Peace Memorial Park, hypnotized by the museum's history of war, nuclear devastation—charred bicycles, charred skin—my wife looks up. We wonder at the acres of *aogiri*—Chinese parasol trees—grown now so large. Half a century later, shielding earth again from the sky's great fire.

Genbaku Dome

Hiroshima's A-Bomb Dome is made of brick, designed by the Czech architect Jan Letzel in 1915. It housed government offices till "Little Boy" fell from the *Enola Gay* in 1945, the dome somehow stubbornly surviving. As I stare, lost in thought, a voice calls out, *Dane, is that you?* A friend from my past, who ambles by from America at this exact moment. You never know what will happen. A shadow, a flash of light, a greeting.

Bamboo Prayers

While resting on a park bench—exhausted by history—across from Hiroshima's A-Bomb Dome memorial, my wife and I are approached by a cheerful old Japanese man in a bright red shirt, walking an antique bike. He asks if he can practice English conversation with us—it's his homework. We mime some words, he sounds out others. He seems a secret Zen master, deflecting our apologies for the war and the bomb. *We are friends*, he says, *it is the war generals we should fear*. At the end, he hands us each a bamboo prayer stick with black calligraphy: pictograms for *peace* and *family*. The A-Bomb Dome hunches like a dark dream across the river.

Presidential Mask

Wandering the vast shopping malls of Kyoto, my wife darts into a small shop, poses next to a contorted rubber mask of Trump, all grimace and orange hair. It is a macabre likeness, not unlike any mask of power. Even the shoguns might be impressed with its snarl. But the centuries make a caricature of power, and even a president may find his head stuck like a mannikin in some lost stall of the world.

The Way Change Happens

For instance, the novelty of leather stirrups advanced warfare, toppled empires, allowed romantic love to conquer the British Isles in the twelfth century. Before, lovers and warriors alike would too often fall off their horses.

Then farmers, tinkering with plows and harnesses, began to plant a third-season crop of protein-rich beans, which fortified the brain at the end of the Dark Ages. Some historians believe this ushered in the Renaissance.

The sway of history—determined by stirrups, beans.

The Museum of Dark Dreams

Two ravens—large as small dogs—canvas the Japanese stone monuments adjacent to the Legion of Honor museum in San Francisco. One looks directly at me, eye to eye. As if to gauge my intention as it scavenges the ground for seeds. Such dark monuments. War still inside our DNA. Calligraphy etched in granite, to remember. The ravens, watching.

Love Poem

The stone in her palm had never been held by hands so soft. It knew hands of briny storm, of tectonic cataclysms, knuckles of whitewater battering the shores rocky till the stone split, fell small against eons of sand and salt polishing its jaggedness smooth. It had been a long, blind journey—the tumult a kind of Braille, a kind of sex. Then nothing. For longer than the stone could remember. But it would remember this briefest of moments. When it lingered in her soft palm—then, poised between thumb and rough finger, was tossed beneath the dark waters. Lived—the way a stone, once touched, lives.

Visiting the Monastery

Camaldoli Hermitage near Big Sur

There is no end to the waves as they sound up this high ridge, and someone in the hermitage is puttering, rustling. Yet the silence grows with each calming roar of wave. How does this happen? My ears grow deaf to worry, listen into this different silence like a deer pausing mid-bite, ears twitching, arching, nostrils alert to the scent of something moving inside the forest.

Breath

In the High Sierra, there are moments of no-sound. No-wind, no-birds rustling in the scrum of trees between granite boulders. I quiet even my breath, lest it sound like a locomotive chugging through the tunnels of lung and throat, the shrill whistle of the nose.

The Fence, the Field, and the Sky

Silence is a field—and there are fences protecting it. As I climb in, amble the perimeter, my hand jostles the fence posts, makes sure they're firm. Eye the straight line of that fence as it runs steady for a long stretch, then angles and angles again till I am surrounded. I linger beside this fence for only a moment—appreciate its rough texture. The boundary of it. The discipline. Then turn, walk into the fenced field's wideness, find a center. Lie down in the soft grass, spread my limbs. Become sky.

Joy's Cliff

The plum isn't very big, dangling from the cliff side—my hand clenching the wiry branch with all its might, other hand reaching for the plum's fiery orb. How did I get here, in this old Zen koan? One tiger standing above on the cliff lip, breath close enough to feel the furnace of, saliva like rain. Below, just like the story, another tiger roars at his good fortune: this easy meal falling from the sky. The koan, I know, is not a test. It is joy's cliff. Someone will be happy here. Likely to be a tiger. In the meantime, I bite the plum, hard. Taste the pulp of it, the purple-black sweet on every bud of my tongue. Someone will be happy here. It might as well be me.

In the Zendo, All Doors Open

Silence. Roshi begins his talk, "Great understanding . . ." As if on cue, a loud toilet flush. A few moments later, "Great words . . ." and, impossibly, a second loud *whoosh!* Everyone now wide awake.

ACKNOWLEDGMENTS

Sixteen Rivers Press encompasses the bioregion many of these poems occur in. The California coast is also part of the Pacific Rim stretching to Asia and back—a key influence in my family history and on my work. I am grateful for the support the press has provided to bring this book into being. I also want to thank my longtime Santa Cruz writing group, the Emerald Street Writers, whose gracious attentions have helped many of these poems take shape over the years. And I would like to express my love and appreciation for my family and dear friends, without whom this life and these poems would not exist.

Grateful acknowledgment to the following publications, in which these poems first appeared:

- *Ambush Review*: "The Birth of the Modern World," "Self-Abuse in the Victorian Age"

- *Caesura*: "The World Is God's Language"

- *Ginosko Literary Journal*: "Old World," "Communion," "Mystery of the Locked Door," "Secret Lover"

- *LALITAMBA*: "The Empty Hand Holds the World," "Do I Wake or Sleep?"

- *Loose Leaf Tea*: "Anti-Mass"

- *Monterey Poetry Review*: "The Dreams of Antelope," "The Unseen," "Breast," "The Second Coming," "Eros Finds a Way"

- *PROEM*: "The Way Change Happens," "Broken Desire," "Dinosaurs"

- *Prometheus Dreaming*: "Shaking Penises"

- *r-kv-r-y*: "The Measure of Desire," "Keeping Watch"

- *Rock & Sling*: "Salvation's Weight," "Some Prayers Are Better Left Unanswered," "The Foot-Washing Ceremony"

- *The Broken Bridge Review*: "Strange Calculus," "Looking Forward," "Magellan's Voyage Around the World"

- *The Dewdrop*: "Growing Old," "Practicing," "World Yoga," "The Third Face of God," "Surprise!"

"The Anthropology of Memory" was published in *The Original Van Gogh's Ear Anthology*. "The Parable of St. Matthew Island" and "The Dreams of Antelope" were published in *Ghost Fishing: An Eco-Justice Poetry Anthology* (University of Georgia Press).

NOTES

The poems in the first chronological arc of this book occur in the "fertile triangle" between central California's San Joaquin Valley and the nearby Sierra Mountains, the San Francisco Bay Area, and the coastal town of Santa Cruz where I've lived for many years.

___

The setting for some of the early family poems shifts between two sites: Sandy Acres, my childhood home of nine acres just outside the small town of Atwater, and Shangri-La, my parents' thirty-eight acre property just outside Mariposa on the way to Yosemite, named for the mystical site in my father's favorite childhood book, *Lost Horizons*. My parents built a "little village" of six hexagonal structures of varying sizes there as a place of retreat for family and friends. Our friends Peter and Ronda built their own rustic cabin on the adjacent hill, where later my Uncle David and Aunt Suzanne built a home on the same site. We came and went from Shangri-La many times over the years, a place of retreat for family and friends alike.

___

My father, while stationed in Japan during the Korean War, fell in love with all things Japanese. I was raised in dusty, conservative central California with Japanese architecture and gardens, decks, and bonsai plants. This Japanese influence likely led to my later immersion in Buddhism and the practice of mindfulness. Though he began his career as a Christian minister, he and my mother became public school teachers in Atwater before retiring to the mountains in pursuit of the New Age. My mother also ran a metaphysical book and gift store downtown called Synchronicity for twenty years after she retired.

Travel poems and encounters with cultures other than one's "own" are now suspect for several good reasons, colonialism and its shadowed legacies among them. When I travel, I attempt to be mindful of these shadows—and more importantly, to be humbled by all I encounter: people, history, geography, politics. On this theme, I was struck by the words of editor Sandra Meek in the anthology *Deep Travel: Contemporary American Poets Abroad*:

> At times, the charge of appropriation has been flung more generally at all "travel writing," all writing of "the other." But at the very foundation of this position lie troubling assumptions: that any engagement with other cultures, with other landscapes, results in appropriation; that to step out of the known, the familiar, is to overstep one's "proper bounds"; that art begins from a space of authority and mastery, rather than from uncertainty, from a humble and generative openness to discovery.

My hope is that the poems in this collection will be read in this spirit of discovery.

"The Third Face of God": In Hinduism, the triune god is Brahma as creator, Vishnu as preserver, and Shiva as destroyer.

"Joy's Cliff": In other versions of this story, the fruit is a strawberry, not a plum.

The World Is God's Language is a call to listen. The divine speaks through the world in all its variety, not only the monastic, according to author Dane Cervine. Pairs of prose poems attuned to the sensibility of the koan contemplate family, the psych ward, the carnal, ritual, remembrance, history and its silences. The poems extend through time and around the planet, like picaresque parables that embrace the wide world. Cervine's deft juxtaposition of mystery and the ordinary renders poems of satisfying paradox and surprising insight that are gratifying to read and read again.

—**SALLY ASHTON**, author of *The Behaviour of Clocks*

Dane Cervine's poems cast their attention on the everyday—his father's slippers, an orange cat, the last biscuit in a box—and find the extraordinary in what's in front of all of us. Even when the poems take place in distant locales, Cervine makes magic with simplicity. Hand in hand, he takes his readers to the edge, and willingly, we jump with him.

—**PATRICE VECCHIONE**, author of *My Shouting, Shattered, Whispering Voice: A Guide to Writing Poetry & Speaking Your Truth*

Dane Cervine's new book, *The World Is God's Language*, is a raft for troubled souls, a balm for aching hearts, and a tree of koan-like wisdom nuggets to be squirreled away and returned to again and again. These prose poems often address loss and difficulties but with a lightness of touch that emphasizes the spiritual lessons they can embody. In one, the speaker tells us: "my wandering brother buys a house . . . caresses the timbers . . . like a lover. Like a body he could spend the rest of his life inside." Ultimately, it is this kind of acceptance and wonder these poems teach. Another reports a conversation: "*I'm practicing dying,* he said to his daughter in his last days. *I slowly stop breathing to see what it's like, then let go.* His words almost eager: *I think I can do this*—the way a young boy steadies himself on the cliff bank over a river, gnarled rope in hand, leaps." Dane Cervine steadies us with his attention to each word, his deceptive simplicity of language, and his calibrated spirituality—which outlines mysteries, rather than attempting to fill them in. These remarkable poems are Rumi-like pearls.

—**DAVID SULLIVAN**, author of *Seed Shell Ash*

Sixteen Rivers Press is a shared-work, nonprofit poetry collective
dedicated to providing an alternative publishing avenue for
San Francisco Bay Area poets. Founded in 1999 by seven writers,
the press is named for the sixteen rivers
that flow into San Francisco Bay.

SAN JOAQUIN · FRESNO · CHOWCHILLA · MERCED · TUOLUMNE
STANISLAUS · CALAVERAS · BEAR · MOKELUMNE · COSUMNES · AMERICAN
YUBA · FEATHER · SACRAMENTO · NAPA · PETALUMA